Introductio

The average visitor to a British seaside resort in 1987 might be forgiven for thinking that the remains of the British Seaside Pier had only been there for entertainment.

One only has to look back less than thirty years as some of the photographs in this book prove when regular calls were made at a goodly number of seaside piers by what one would term full size excursion vessels and not the 'florry boats' which economics and the rise of the motor car have forced on most places.

But to assume that the paddle steamers which could be seen hanging on to the end of such piers as Brighton, Mumbles, and Clacton were there purely for pleasure and had been since time immemorial would be wrong.

In 1812, the paddle steamer 'Comet' started the first commercially successful steamboat service from Glasgow to Port Glasgow. This operation sowed the seed which was to blossom into the steamer fleets of late nineteenth century.

Services in those early days were primarily to get people from A to B as shipboard travel was much faster than road, and in many cases more direct. The coming of the railways changed all this. The steamers were forced to connect with the trains at firth piers. Inevitably the fleets came under railway control, and not only on the Clyde, but where ferry services as an extension to train journeys were necessary throughout the British Isles paddle steamers filled the bill.

As ships grew in size and comfort, it was natural that they attracted 'day trippers' who simply took a sail for pleasure. As this market developed the owners responded by building larger vessels purely aimed at the cruise market. But the overwhelming need was still for a means of crossing those wide river estuaries and getting to island outposts round our coasts.

Competition forced some operators out of business, and others moved to new ground. P. & A. Campbell for example started operations on the Clyde, but due to the upsurge in Railway competition moved one vessel to the Bristol Channel, in 1887. This resulted in a total move to Bristol in 1889 and the development of one of the largest fleets of excursion vessels in UK waters.

The railway companies' fleets continued to expand and many were operating in direct competition with each other. On the Clyde, the Caledonian Steam Packet Co., (a separate company was necessary to operate ships due to legislation restricting the scope and destinations of services by railway owned boats) the Glasgow & South Western Railway, and the North British Railway all vied with each other for trade. It was traditional for many Glasgow businessmen to own or rent a summer house at one of the Clyde resorts. This entailed commuting to the city every day. Steamer services were run to strict timetables in connection with fast trains from the coastal piers and racing was rife!

The First World War saw many of the vessels taken over by the Royal Navy and commissioned as minesweepers. It is interesting to note that the success of the conversions led to the Admiralty having a whole fleet of Racecourse Class Paddle Minesweepers built. There were a goodly number of old favourites lost as a result of hostilities. Strange to say only two of the Racecourse class were sold for civilian use.

Postwar revival took some time, as a number of the piers were no longer fit to use after hostilities ceased — others had gone altogether. New vessels were ordered, partly paid for by government compensation.

Things were never really to be the same again. The railways were grouped into four companies in 1923 and erstwhile competitors hoisted the same houseflags. The upsurge of motor traffic in the thirties caused some vessels to be built to accommodate cars, eg, Red Funnel's Gracie Fields and the Humber 'Castles'. But the attractions of the motor car and road transport were to spell the end of the excursion trade in due course.

For ferry work, motorships and screw propellors took over. Only where because of its shallow draft, manoevreability, and stopping power a paddler was more desirable did they continue to be built for ferry work. The major owners had up-to-date vessels with deck saloons built in the thirties to replace worn out tonnage, and the world's first diesel electric direct drive vessel 'Talisman' appeared on the scene.

Even by the advent of World War Two in 1939 some owners had vessels laid up for want of work. Nevertheless once again the paddlers donned admiralty grey and went minesweeping and later were used as anti-aircraft vessels. Some did not come back; indeed many of them gave their finest hours when Dunkirk was evacuated in 1940.

Those vessels which did return faced an uncertain future. Some new tonnage was built and vast (for those days!) expenditure was incurred in virtually rebuilding others after war service, fortunately paid for in the main by compensation. Whilst two new paddle steamers were built for Bristol Channel use, and one was built for the Clyde other concerns turned to screw propulsion, eg The Southern Railway replaced its two war losses with twin screw motorships.

The fifties was entered with the railways having been nationalised in 1948 and their associated shipping also came under this umbrella. On the Clyde a programme of replacing paddle and turbine vessels with smaller motorships and car ferries was embarked upon to meet changing needs. By the end of the decade many old favourites had succumbed not only through old age but through the economical fact that they were too costly to run and maintain, and there weren't the passengers around to support them as they took to their motor cars by the thousand. Even vessels converted to burn fuel from the same sources as that of the motor vehicles which helped to hasten their end succumbed. Some had been converted after the war, the general trend on the Clyde was a conversion programme in the mid-1950s, yet other areas never saw oil burners.

The sixties saw further retrenchment and at the end of that decade the Bristol Channel, Thames, and South Coast were without paddle tonnage. By 1970 only Waverley was left in operation on the Clyde, and the three coal burners on the Humber. Some vessels escaped the cutters torch to become floating pubs and restaurants.

This left 'Waverley' as the only real sea-going vessel and in 1973 she was withdrawn also. What has happened since is another story but suffice to say that all readers of this book should support her as she continues as the **Last Seagoing Paddle Steamer in the World.** Economics dictate that she visits as many of the places where the old favourites seen in these following pages once plied; that is where piers or jetties can still accommodate her. As I write this it is sad to hear that she has suffered a spell of 'boiler sickness' which has curtailed her 1987 season. It is to be hoped that this can be cured and that she will sail on!

1

1. The Broomielaw Glasgow, was the starting point for many of the Clyde vessels for most of the nineteenth century. Here, the spartan accommodation of the flush decked vessels of the 'seventies is seen.

2. The *Edinburgh Castle* was built for the Lochgoil & Lochlong Steamboat Company in 1879. Features of note are the large paddleboxes with the bridge between them, and the narrow saloon aft. After passing to Turbine Steamers Ltd., in 1912 she only operated for them for two seasons and was broken up in 1913. Built by Duncan of Port Glasgow and engined with a single diagonal engine by Rankine & Blackmore.

3. Lochgoilhead pier with the North British *Marmion* of 1906 double-berthed alongside *Edinburgh Castle. Marmion* was the second NB paddler to have compound diagonal engines and the first to have the bridge ahead of the funnel.

4. The NB flagship *Waverley,* built in 1899 calling at Whiting Bay, Isle of Arran probably in the 1900 season. Note the horse brakes in the foreground — it is easy to forget that the horse reigned supreme on our roads in those days.

5. The *Lord of the Isles* (1891) calls at Rothesay on her daily run from Glasgow to Inveraray.

2

3

4

5

6

7

8

9

6. North bank railhead. North British steamers await the rail connection at from Glasgow at Craigendoran. The vessel nearest the camera is the *Kenilworth* of 1898.

7. South bank railhead. The Caledonian Steam Packet Co's *Duchess of Rothesay* at Princes Pier, Greenock, in the late thirties, with the recently built Marchioness of Lorne just leaving the next berth.

8. Departure. The Williamson Buchanan steamer *Kylemore* leaving Dunoon. This steamer had an interesting history, having been sold whilst fitting out to the Hastings, St Leonards-on-sea and Eastbourne Steamboat Company to become *Britannia.* She spent a time from 1904-08 sailing as *Vulcan* of the Glasgow & South Western fleet, and finally returned to Captain John Williamson's fleet as *Kylemore.*

9. *Benmore* was built at Rutherglen in 1876 for Campbell's Kilmun trade and sailed for them until sold to Captain Buchanan in 1885. She was a typical 'raised quarter deck' steamer of the period with the main deck aft being level with the top of the hull plating rather than having bulwarks aft. This gave more headroom in the saloon. She was sold to Captain Buchanan in 1892, ran for the CSP Co., during the First World War, and in 1920 was damaged by fire, being finally broken up at Dumbarton in 1923.

10. A deck view of the 'teetotal' *Ivanhoe,* built for the Firth of Clyde S.P. Co. Ltd., in 1880, who operated her until 1894 with no bars on board selling alcohol. After a spell on the Manchester Ship Canal she returned to join the CSP Clyde fleet in 1897. In 1911 she again passed into private hands and finally joined the fleet of Turbine Steamers Ltd., in 1914. She was originally well known for the Arran via the Kyles of Bute run and the view gives the impression of what steamer travel was like on the early boats when the rain came on prior to the provision of deck shelters.

10

11. The *Lord of the Isles* was built by D. & W. Henderson of Partick to replace an earlier steamer of the same name in 1891. Her oscillating machinery was somewhat outdated for that time, but she maintained the Inveraray service of the Glasgow & Inveraray Steamboat Co., until 1912 when sold to Turbine Steamers Ltd. She still sailed from Glasgow, but principally round the Island of Bute.

In her last season she spent some time on the Lochgoilhead and Arrochar run in replacement of *Iona*, but was condemned at the end of that season. She kept her attractive red funnels with black and white bands till the end, and is seen here in Bowling Harbour, a place well known at one time as a lay-up berth for those Clyde steamers which did not operate all the year round.

12. The Caledonian Steam Packet Co's, colour scheme whilst under Caledonian Railway control was most attractive, and is seen here on the 1902 *Duchess of Montrose* built by John Brown of Clydebank. The hull was deep blue with green boot topping, and the saloons were pink, set off against a buff funnel and white paddleboxes. The machinery in this and other contemporary CSP vessels was of the two crank, triple expansion diagonal type, with two sets of cylinders in tandem. The *Montrose* was lost whilst minesweeping off the Belgian coast in 1917, and her name is probably better known on her successor, the turbine of 1930.

13. In contrast, the Glasgow & South Western Railway's colour scheme followed along much the same lines as that of the Union Castle Line, with lavender grey hulls, red funnel with black top, and white upperworks. The *Glen Rosa* seen here was one of three vessels to the same design, the second being sold to the Belfast & County Down Railway as *Slieve Donard. Glen Rosa* was the third, and from 1891 was employed on summer excursions and winter ferry work which she continued to perform, with little incident, until her scrapping in 1939.

14 & 15. The big *Juno* it is said, came into the GSW fleet secondhand, being initially ordered for work on the south coast. In the two pictures here she is seen in original GSW livery, and the later LMS livery in the lower. She was best known for her excursion work from Ayr and remained on this station until her withdrawal and scrapping at Alloa in 1931-2, apart from a spell running from the GSW base in 1919 after she had been minesweeping as HMS Junior since 1914.

13

15

16

17

18

16. The first vessel ordered by the Caledonian Steam Packet Company was the 1889 *Caledonia,* built by John Reid & Co., of Port Glasgow, and the predecessor of the well known 1934 vessel of the same name. She had compound machinery but with two cylinders in tandem driving the same crank. Like most of the early steamers her bridge was abaft of the funnel, but this was moved in front on re-boilering in 1903. After a spell of minesweeping in the 1914-18 war, she returned to her old haunts until withdrawn in 1933.

17. A further shot of *Glen Rosa,* this time in LMS colours, taken on the 17th August 1937.

18. The *Jupiter* was built for the Glasgow & South Western Railway fleet by John Brown of Clydebank in 1896. Seen here on the 15th June, 1935, she spent her last years on the Wemyss Bay-Millport run from Wemyss Bay, being withdrawn in 1935.

19 & 20. Two shots of the CSP Co's *Duchess of Rothesay* taken in the thirties, the lower one with winter boarding in place forward. The *Rothesay* was built by J. & G. Thomson at Clydebank in 1895 and she had compound diagonal engines with steam coming from a double ended boiler with the flues designed to exhaust up one funnel. She saw service in both wars, but was too worn out to recondition in 1945 and was broken up in Holland.

21

21 & 22. The best looking and longest lived of the C.S.P. Co., *Duchess* trio was the graceful *Duchess of Fife* built by Fairfields in 1903. Her two crank triple expansion engines supplied from two forced draught navy boilers made her a most economical 'all-year-round' boat. She survived two World Wars and after being virtually rebuilt in 1945 was withdrawn in 1953.

22

23 & 24. The LMS and its associated Caledonian Steam Packet Company took delivery of replacement tonnage in the thirties. The *Mercury* was built by Fairfields in 1934 and a new feature was the enclosed style of paddle box. Triple expansion three crank machinery supplied by a single boiler was fitted and other modern features were the deck shelters, two masts, and a large, eliptical funnel. The vessel is seen prior to her launch and approaching Gourock in the lower shot. Requisitioned for minesweeping in 1939, she was lost on Christmas Day, 1940.

25. Better known than *Mercury* was *Caledonia* also built in 1934 by Denny of Dumbarton. She was not an exact sister, having many detail differences and two navy boilers. She served as *Goatfell* from 1939-45, and was the second last paddle steamer in the CSP fleet, being withdrawn in 1969. Preserved on the Thames as a floating 'pub' she was sadly damaged by fire in 1980 and sold for breaking up — her engines survive however!

She is seen here at Ardrishaig in the 'blue hull' era imposed on the Clyde fleet in 1965.

23

24

25

26

26. By the thirties the 'all the way' sailings left from Bridge Wharf on the south side of the Clyde. Here *Eagle III* is seen about to leave for a trip 'doon the watter.'

27. *Eagle III* was the last Clyde steamer to be powered by a single diagonal engine and haystack boiler. Built in 1910 by Napier & Miller she initially proved to be unstable and extensive hull modifications were required. Although she survived both World Wars she was deemed not worthy of reconditioning after World War II, and scrapped in 1946.

28. *Isle of Arran* was built by Seath of Rutherglen for the Glasgow-Arran run of Buchanan Steamers Ltd., she was a typical steamer of the 1890s having the fore-saloon carried out to just aft of the mast. After a long career, latterly on the Rothesay service, she was sold to southern owners in 1933. (see plate 84)

29. Another shot of *Kylemore* heading down firth on 17th July 1937.

30. The *Queen Empress* entered the Williamson fleet in 1912 and was built by Murdoch and Murray of Port Glasgow. With compound diagonal engines and two navy boilers she followed the design of the CSP ships of the period, in which fleet she finished her peacetime career from 1936. Serving in both World Wars she was found unfit for reconditioning in 1945 and was sold for scrap. The funnel colours of the Williamson and later the Williamson Buchanan fleets were white with a black top.

27

28

29

30

31. The 1899 *Waverley* was the flagship of the North bank fleet which after 1923 came under LNER control. She is seen here on the 12th May 1937 in her latterday condition with deck saloons fore and aft and the grey hull introduced to the Craigendoran fleet in 1936. She was lost whilst assisting in the evacuation of Dunkirk on 29th May 1940. With all the publicity surrounding the discovery of the wreck of the *Titanic* it is interesting to note that the remains of *Waverley* were found recently by a French diver.

32. *Marmion* was built by Inglis of Pointhouse, builders of most NB steamers, in 1906 and was essentially a smaller version of *Waverley* as built but with bridge forward of the funnel from the outset. For minesweeping work in 1915 her promenade deck was extended to the bows in this form she proved unsuitable for passenger service on return to the NB fleet in 1920. In 1923 she was altered to the condition shown in the photograph. She was badly damaged by bombing at Harwich in April 1941 and subsequently scrapped.

33 to 35. *Jeanie Deans* was bult by Fairfields of Govan for the LNER Fleet in 1931 and was the first Clyde vessel to have triple expansion, three crank diagonal engines. She also sported a double ended boiler and originally, two rather short funnels.

She is seen in plate 33 in the late thirties after her funnels had been heightened, but not equally. Requisitioned for war service in 1939 when she returned to Clyde service in 1946 she looked very different as seen in plate 34. Our final picture is one taken at Craigendoran in the early sixties with *Waverley* astern. The similarity in appearance of the two vessels can be seen in this shot, *Jeanie* having been reconditioned along the lines of Waverley as originally envisaged. A popular ship, her withdrawal in 1964 saw her sold for further service — see plate 92.

33

34

35

36 to 38. *Talisman* was unique in paddle steamer circles in being powered by direct drive diesel electric machinery — her outer appearance belied this. She is seen in virtually original condition in plate 36, the excursion advertised must have been one of the few occasions she used her Class III certificate (excursion to sea in fine weather). She became HMS *Aristocrat* in 1940 after a somewhat chequered pre-war career. After reconditioning she appeared in 1946 somewhat altered in accord with the style of the two steam units of the LNER fleet, and survived until 1966, latterly on the Millport service, having been re-engined in 1954.

39 to 41. *Waverley* was the only steamer built for Clyde service after World War II and appeared in 1947. In plate 39 she is seen on arrival from the builders in 1947 with *Lucy Ashton* (1888). Her modern history is well known since 'preservation' so we show two shots of her, plate 40 under CSP control in 1958 leaving Gourock on a schools charter, and sporting the new Caledonian MacBrayne colours in May 1973.

Lucy Ashton had a long and distinguished Clyde career, she sailed on the Clyde during both wars, and was successfully modernised, being re-engined with compound diagonals in 1902. She finally ended Clyde service in her sixtieth year.

36

Glasgow Grocers' & Provision Merchants' Excursion Committee.

THE THIRTY-SIXTH

EXCURSION

Promoted by this Committee will take place

On TUESDAY, 16th JUNE, 1936,

Per Magnificent Diesel-Electric Vessel

"TALISMAN."

To BRODICK

Via Largs Channel and Garrochhead, returning by Kyles of Bute.

Tickets (Adults) 12/6 *(including Dinner & High Te*

Juveniles (under 10) 6/6

Juvenile Tickets can only be had direct from the Secretary

37

38

(40)

(41)

42. MacBrayne's *Iona* dated back to 1864 and replaced a previous vessel of the same name sold for blockade running. She spent most of her time on the Clyde services of her owners and had a very long life not being withdrawn until 1936. She spent most summers from 1927 at Oban and replaced *Columba* on the Ardrishaig run at the beginning and end of each season. Her simple machinery speeded her demise and she retained her narrow deck saloons to the end, these having been replaced in 1919.

43. The celebrated *Columba* dated from 1878 and was well known for years serving the 'Royal Route' from Glasgow to Ardrishaig. David MacBrayne Ltd., operated some Clyde services, and indeed that company from 1928 had been partly owned by the LMS Railway Co., and Coast Lines.

The Columba enjoyed an almost eternal youth, and despite being somewhat outdated with her twin cylinder, non compound oscillating machinery, this served her well right up to withdrawal in 1936 when the sheer economics of operating such a large and outdated ship overtook her. This shot shows her graceful lines with one funnel forward and one aft of the paddles.

44. *Chevalier* was built in 1866 and was a smaller edition of *Iona.* She shared most characteristics of the larger vessel, and spent most of her seasonal existence on the Corpach to Crinan route calling at Fort William, and Oban. Sometimes relieving on the Clyde she met her end after running ashore in a gale whilst on the Ardrishaig run in March 1927 following a paddle wheel failure. She was salvaged but broken up.

45. *Fusilier* completes our look at MacBraynes vessels and was built in 1888. Her machinery departed at last from the oscillating machinery used on earlier vessels, having a single diagonal engine with steam from a haystack boiler. She is seen here in latterday condition with bridge moved forward of a heightened funnel. Spending most of her life at Oban, being used variously on the Iona and Fort William services she was sold in 1934 and her further wanderings are decribed under plate 103.

46

46. We now move to a different coastal environment, that of the BristolChannel, where tidal ranges require the style of pier seen here in the background at Weston-Super-Mare with one of the Campbells' steamers leaving. Here is a case of seaside amusements sharing the scene with a landing stage for steamer services. For many years P. & A. Campbell operated a Cardiff-Weston ferry service in the summer season.

47. The similarity of the earlier Bristol Channel paddler to its Clyde cousins is to be noted in this shot of *Ravenswood,* built in 1891 at Ayr. She is seen in original condition with two haystack boilers running down the Severn Bore from Bristol on the Ilfracombe service. She had a long life, not being withdrawn until 1955. Her final condition is seen in Plate 48 showing the enclosed paddle boxes fitted after reconditioning following wartime minesweeping by Chas. Hill of Bristol in 1945.

49. *Waverley* was in fact built for Campbell's Clyde services in 1885, and, following a charter in the 1887 season on the Bristol Channel, she commenced operations there in 1888. She is seen here in later condition prior to the 1914-18 War, at Eastbourne; she often operated on the South Coast after Campbell's moved some of their operations there. She was not reconditioned after war service. A single diagonal engine received steam from a haystack boiler.

50. *Westward Ho!* was also an Ayr built steamer and entered service in 1894. She was the first Campbell vessel to have the promenade deck carried right to the bows. She was fitted with compound diagonal engines from the outset. Ports instead of windows were fitted to the saloons in 1920, and she served in both wars, being broken up in 1946. She operated on most White Funnel services in her time.

47

48

49

50

51. Serious competition came to the Bristol Channel in 1905 with the entry of the Barry Railway Company to the scene. *Gwalia* was built by John Brown of Clydebank in 1905 and entered service in striking colours of grey hull and red funnels with black tops. Compound diagonal engines and a double ended boiler were fitted. She was sold in 1910 to the Furness Railway and renamed *Lady Moyra* returning to the Bristol Channel after war service in 1918, under the ownership of Tuckers of Cardiff. In 1922 she joined the Campbell fleet, and was renamed *Brighton Queen* in 1933, being thenceforward employed mainly on the south coast. She was lost whilst helping in the evacuation of Dunkirk.

52. *Devonia* of 1905 was an almost identical sister but came into Campbell hands in time for the 1912 season. She is seen here in original condition as sailing for the Barry Railway, and in plate 53 in later Campbell condition. Note the extra lifeboats added after the *Titanic* disaster in 1912 and the general refurbishment undertaken to give her the typical Campbell appearance. She was also lost in the Dunkirk evacuation in 1940.

54. *Glen Avon* was built by Ailsa of Troon in 1912 and represented the 'standard' design of steamer supplied to the Campbell fleet and copied by others. She had an uneventful career, which ended whilst on war service in 1944. The use of the work 'Glen' is interesting as the Avon Valley is not so called, but this had no doubt something to do with the Scottish origins of the Campbell fleet.

55. Built in 1907 by John Brown of Clydebank for the Barry Railway Co., as *Barry* she appeared when new with the NB funnel colours of red funnel with white band and black top. She joined the Campbell fleet in 1911, and following reconditioning at the Ailsa yard after war service in 1920, she returned to the White Funnel fleet, being renamed *Waverley* in 1926. She was sent to the South Coast station at this time and as with other steamers used there, a bow rudder was fitted to aid maneouvrability when backing off such piers as Brighton, Eastbourne, and Hastings. She was sunk whilst again on war service in July 1941.

53

54

55

56
ENGINEERS & SHIPBUILDERS
57
58

59

56 to 58. *Britannia* was built in 1896 at Ayr, and the three plates here show part of her interesting history. Plate 56 shows her at Barclay Curle's year on the Clyde after reboilering in 1935 when she received a larger, eliptical funnel. She is seen in this guise in plate 57.

After war service boiler trouble caused her to be fitted with a new double ended boiler which required the use of two funnels, and she is seen landing passengers at Clovelly. This practice of ferrying passengers ashore was commonplace on the Bristol Channel where there were no piers. *Britannia* was sold for scrapping in 1956.

59. *Glen Usk* was built in 1914 might be described as the most economical paddler that Campbells owned. She had a long life, and served in both wars lasting until 1963. Latterly she was laid up, and plans were afoot to convert her to oil firing, but these never materialised.

60. *Glen Gower* made her appearance in 1922 and was fitted with the secondhand engines from *Albion*. She spent the immediate pre-war years on the South Coast, and in 1955 started 'no-passport' day trips to France which had ceased with the war in 1939. Latterly laid up she was sold for scrapping in 1960.

60

61

61 and 62. The most famous Bristol Channel paddle steamer of recent memory was *Bristol Queen*. She came from Charles Hill's Bristol year in 1946 and was the first ship for Campbells to be built there. Her triple diagonal engines were supplied by Rankin and Blackmore of Greenock and were virtually identical to those of the 1947 *Waverley*. She was an oil burner from the outset. The photographs were both taken in the sixties, plate 61 shows her leaving Ilfracombe astern, and plate 62 landing passengers by boat at Lundy. *Bristol Queen* was herself laid up in 1959 and 1960, but was returned to service in 1961. She failed to end the 1967 season due to paddle damage, and was subsequently put up for sale and went to Belgium for scrap in 1968. She was built with subdivision to allow her use on cross-Channel excursions on which she never appeared, although she did regularly visit the Scilly Isles.

62

63

63 and 64. Campbells were well pleased with *Bristol Queen* and went back to Hills for a second vessel. Hills were faced with a full order book and could not handle the job, so the building of the second ship went out to tender. Inglis offered a modified version of *Waverley* and Fairfields a modified version of the 1937 LMS *Juno and Jupiter*. In the event, Fairfields got the contract on delivery terms, and the result was *Cardiff Queen*. She was readily identifiable from her big sister by having a teak bridge surround. Our photographs show her leaving Bideford and a stern view leaving Penarth. She was withdrawn and put up for sale in 1966 and after various abortive projects for further use was scrapped in 1968.

64

65

65 and 66. We now move to the South Coast, and to the operating area of the cumbersome Southampton, Isle of Wight & South of England Royal Mail Steam Packet Company Ltd. In addition to operating steamer services the concern operated tugs, and still operates these along with car ferries. The *Princess Elizabeth,* built by Day, Summers, of Southampton in 1927 was designed to carry motor vehicles on her open foredeck. In plate 65 she is seen in her original condition with narrow saloon and alleyways.

Plate 66 shows her latterday condition, arriving at Cowes. Note the bulwark doors open ready to unload the cars on board at the pontoon. After withdrawal and sale, an abortive attempt to operate her from Torquay in 1960 started a chequered career sailing firstly from Bournemouth and later Weymouth. She is now moored on the Thames upriver from Tower Bridge, engine and boilerless, and is in use as a floating pub.

66

67. After buying motorship tonnage in 1931, the Southampton Co., went back to paddles and steam propulsion in 1936, and *Gracie Fields* was launched by the well known singer! Very similar to *Princess Elizabeth* but with built up forecastle, *Gracie* had a short career, being sunk whilst assisting with the evacuation of Dunkirk in 1940.

68. *Lord Elgin* had the distinction of being the last cargo paddle vessel in service in UK water. She started life as a passenger steamer on the Forth, being built at Stockton on Tees in 1876. She came south to Bournemouth in 1881 and passed to the Southampton Co., in 1909. She became a cargo steamer in 1911 and operated the Southampton to Cowes cargo service, latterly as spare steamer, until withdrawn and scrapped in 1955.

70

71

72

69 to 71. *Balmoral* was built for the Southampton Co., to compete with Campbell's *Cumbria.* She was built at McKnight's yard at Ayr and was driven by a powerful set of compound diagonal engines. When entering service in 1900 she carried a white funnel as seen, at Southampton, in plate 69. She is seen going 'round yachts during Cowes Week in plate 70, and with red funnel in the thirties in plate 71. She was often employed on Cherbourg daytrips. After the Second World War, *Balmoral* was considered to be in too poor a shape to warrant reconditioning.

72. *Bournemouth Queen* was built for the Southampton Co., by the Ailsa Yard at Troon, entering service in 1908. She was always associated with Bournemouth until 1951 when she became based at Southampton, finally succumbing to the breakers in 1957. She was, in effect, a smaller version of *Balmoral.*

73. *Lorna Doone* was built in 1891 for Edwards, Robertson & Co, of Cardiff and entered the Southampton Co's fleet in 1898. Our illustration shows her in original condition with two funnels. Subsequent re-boilering reduced her funnels to one in number and she was later plated up forward. She had a long career, finishing as an anti-aircraft ship in the 1939-45 War, and meeting the same fate as *Balmoral.*

73

74

75

76

74. *Queen* dated from 1902 and in the thirties suffered two name changes, being re-named *Mauretania* in 1936, and *Corfe Castle* in 1937. She was withdrawn in 1938.

75. We now move to the Weymouth based fleet of Cosens & Co., who operated some rather antique vessels right into the nineteen fifties. Their *Premier* is seen here. She dated back to 1846 and by the time this photograph was taken in the thirties she had been re-engined with single oscillating engines, re-boilered, and lengthened. She was one of the last 'flush decked' vessels to survive in service.

76. One of the features of the Weymouth area was the practice of beaching the steamers on the shallow sloping beaches, such as at Lulworth Cove, seen here. The *Empress* seen here performing the operation with kedge anchors laid out astern, was built on the Thames in 1879 and lasted until 1955. She had the last set of oscillating paddle engines in operation.

77. The first *Monarch* dated from 1888 and was built on the Thames at Blackwall, with a twin diagonal engine by Penn of Greenwich. She operated on the Bournemouth station for over sixty years, being broken up in 1950. Her original appearance was antique to say the least — she sported bell mouthed tops to her funnels.

78. *Emperor of India* started life as the Southampton Co's *Princess Royal* in 1906 and after rejection by that concern she was returned to her builders, who lengthened her and she was subsequently sold to Cosens entering their fleet in 1908. The following winter she underwent more alterations including plating up the promenade deck to the bows. Following war service she was altered almost out of recognition on re-entering Cosen's fleet in 1948, being converted to burn oil. She lasted until the end of the 1956 season and was sold for scrapping early in 1957. She was normally associated with the Bournemouth sailings.

78

79

79. The London & South Western and London Brighton & South Coast railways operated a joint fleet on the Solent, and the *Duchess of Norfolk* seen here was one of two sisters which came from D. & W. Henderson's yard in Glasgow in 1911. She was the normal design for the railway fleet and had a single ended Scotch boiler and compound diagonal engines. She operated on Railway connections from Portsmouth to the Isle of Wight, becoming Cosen's *Embassy* in 1937. She served, as from 1914 to 1918, as a minesweeper from 1939-45. Converted to burn oil on reconditioning in 1946, she lasted in Cosen's fleet until 1967.

80. *Duchess of Fife* was built for the joint fleet in 1899 at Clydebank and ran on railway service until 1929. She was to the standard railway design with short fore saloon, and the after saloon surrounded by alleyways; unlike earlier vessels this was fully enclosed by windows at the hull sides.

81. *Merstone* was built at Dundee by the Caledon Co., for the Southern Railway fleet in 1928. A more modern version of the *Duchesses* she had an enclosed wheelhouse from the outset along with a deckhouse at the base of the funnel. She remained on the Portsmouth to Ryde service during hostilities, when her sister *Portsdown* was sunk. Withdrawn in 1948 she was finally broken up at Newhaven in 1952.

82. *Whippingham* was one of two vessels built at Fairfields of Govan for the Southern Railway in 1930 (the other was *Southsea* lost in 1941) and she was designed for long distance excursions from Portsmouth. Her shape was not unlike the LNER *Jeanie Deans* but she only had a single ended boiler and compound diagonal engines. After war service she sailed on with a few noticeable alterations such as the reduction in the number of windows at main deck level. Coal burning until the end, she was barely capable of eleven knots in her later days, and was withdrawn after the 1962 season and sold for scrap the next year.

83. *Ryde* was the second of two ships ordered from Dennys of Dumbarton to replace obsolete tonnage, and she appeared in 1937. The first was *Sandown* in 1934. They were the first SR steamers to have triple expansion engines and were very much smaller versions of the CSP *Caledonia*. *Ryde* is seen here backing off the pier of her name in her latter years. She lasted in service until 1969 and is now a night club up the Medina on the Isle of Wight.

80

81

82

83

84

84. *Isle of Arran* has appeared before in these pages (plate 28) and she came into the ownership of the General Steam Navigation Co., in 1933. She operated on the dock cruises for the P.L.A., two days a week and ran to Herne Bay and Margate on other days. She is seen here at Ramsgate. She only lasted until after the 1936 season and was sold for scrapping in that year.

85. On moving to the Thames it is again interesting to note the similarity of our first vessel to those in Clyde service. *Golden Eagle* was built for GSN in 1909 by John Browns of Clydebank and was the first of their paddlers to have triple expansion, three crank engines. She sailed from London to Margate and Ramsgate. Her London berth was downstream of London Bridge. After the 1939-45 War she ran from Tower Pier to Southend and Clacton, but was not operated during the 1950 season and sold for breaking in 1951.

86. *Crested Eagle* entered service in 1925 and came from the yard of Samuel White at Cowes. She was a large ship of nearly 300 feet in length and was an oil burner from the outset. As she had to shoot London Bridge to reach Old Swan pier, her low lines are to be noted, along with telescopic funnel and short folding mast. She later ran from Tower Pier and a fixed funnel was substituted. She normally ran to Southend and Clacton also giving cruises from that pier. Her end came at Dunkirk when she was bombed and burnt out.

87. It was possible in the old days to travel from London to Great Yarmouth by steamer, and here an old postcard shot of the 'London Boat' at Yarmouth is included. It has been very difficult to identify the vessel concerned.

88. The New Medway Steam Packet Co., purchased the steamer *Walton Belle* from the East Anglia Steamship Co., in 1925, renaming her *Essex Queen*. She had been built in 1897 and lasted with her new owners until after war service in 1946, when she was sold to Devon owners for service from Torquay. She only lasted two seasons there and was laid up until 1951 and then broken up.

85

86

87

88

89

89 and 90. The New Medway Co., had a new steamer built by Ailsa of Troon for the 1924 season, and she was the first Thames' steamer to be plated up to the bow and have the bridge forward of the funnel. She operated from Chatham across the estuary to Southend and thence to Clacton and Felixstowe.

Medway Queen had a long life, sailing into fame at Dunkirk, and latterly ran from Strood following the closure of Sun Pier, Chatham. She was withdrawn and offered for sale in 1963. Various preservation attempts failed, but she eventually went to the Medina on the Isle of Wight for use as a night club. She deteriorated over the years and was replaced by *Ryde* and eventually reached such a condition that she became waterlogged at high water. She was eventually rescued and taken to Chatham where brave attempts are now being made to preserve her. It is to be hoped that they succeed, as she is the only example left of the classic Clyde-built paddle steamer which graced so many of our estuaries and resorts in the pre-war era.

91. So successful were the paddle steamers requisitioned for war work as minesweepers in 1914-15, that the Royal Navy placed orders in 1915 for 24 purpose-built vessels of the *Ascot* class. They were based on Campbell's *Glen Usk* but had two boilers, one forward and one aft of the engines. A further eight were ordered in 1917. Our illustration shows *HMS Epsom,* built by George Brown Greenock , being broken up in 1922.

92. Following war service, only two of the *Ascot* class were sold for use as passenger excursion vessels. This did not happen until 1928/29 when the New Medway Co, bought *HMS Atherstone* direct from the Royal Navy renaming her *Queen of Kent,* and *HMS Melton* from breakers renaming her *Queen of Thanet.* They were used mainly on cross-channel excursion work from Gravesend, Margate and Clacton. Converted to burn oil and fitted with new paddle wheels in 1931 they continued to operate until laid up for the 1939 season. They served again in the Second World War, and were reconditioned for further service after hostilities ceased. They were both sold to the Southampton Co., in 1948 and *Queen of Kent,* shown here, became *Lorna Doone.* She was sold for scrapping in 1952.

93. The final, or not quite final essay in Thames paddlers came when the Clyde favourite *Jeanie Deans* came south in 1965. Purchased by a band of enthusiasts she was prepared for service on London's river in 1966, and renamed *Queen of the South.* Sadly, lack of operational expertise meant that few sailings were operated in 1966, and a lot more money was spent on her readiness for the 1967 season. Boiler trouble dogged her second season and she finally went to Belgium for breaking in December 1967. The successful visit of *Waverley* to the Thames in 1978 with her uncanny similarity to her quasi-sister showed what could have been done if resources had been channelled in the right direction.

90

92

94

94. The accolade for the ugliest paddle steamers ever to operate in UK waters must go to the *Brocklesby* and *Killingholme* built for the Hull-New Holland service of the Great Central Railway in 1912. *Killingholme,* seen here on cruise work from Grimsby, which one of the steamers undertook every summer, lasted until 1940.

95. Under LNER control from 1923, the New Holland fleet was strengthened by the transfer of the Clyde steamer *Dandie Dinmont* in 1928 to the Humber. She was modified as shown here for her new role, and lasted until 1936. She had the reputation of being the fastest steamer on the ferry run with pier times of 8 minutes being recorded.

95

96

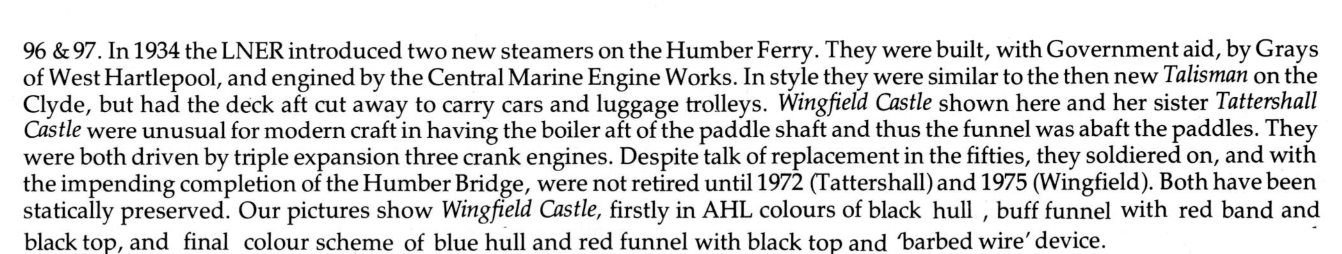

96 & 97. In 1934 the LNER introduced two new steamers on the Humber Ferry. They were built, with Government aid, by Grays of West Hartlepool, and engined by the Central Marine Engine Works. In style they were similar to the then new *Talisman* on the Clyde, but had the deck aft cut away to carry cars and luggage trolleys. *Wingfield Castle* shown here and her sister *Tattershall Castle* were unusual for modern craft in having the boiler aft of the paddle shaft and thus the funnel was abaft the paddles. They were both driven by triple expansion three crank engines. Despite talk of replacement in the fifties, they soldiered on, and with the impending completion of the Humber Bridge, were not retired until 1972 (Tattershall) and 1975 (Wingfield). Both have been statically preserved. Our pictures show *Wingfield Castle,* firstly in AHL colours of black hull , buff funnel with red band and black top, and final colour scheme of blue hull and red funnel with black top and 'barbed wire' device.
Like their predecessors, they were used for cruising from Grimsby in summer, one vessel being stationed there.

97

98

99

100

101

98,99 and 100. A third vessel *Lincoln Castle* joined the two 1934 sisters in 1940, but built by Inglis of Pointhouse. She was more conventional in layout with the funnel forward of the paddles and was engined by the Ailsa Co, of Troon. She outlasted the other pair on account of her being somewhat lighter in build and less powerful, being unsuitable for winter or cruising work, spending much time at the layup berth. Her continued operation until the opening of the bridge was expected, but boiler failure caused her premature withdrawal. She has also been statically preserved, and has recently been moved to a new site at Grimsby.

Our pictures show her in AHL colours leaving New Holland, approaching Corporation Pier at Hull in Sealink colours, and on a charter cruise to Goole turning in the River Ouse.

101. To replace *Wingfield Castle* Sealink moved the Diesel Electric Paddle ferry *Farringford,* built by Denny in 1947 for the Lymington-Yarmouth service of the Southern Railway, to the Humber. She was really unsuited for the job, being deeper in draught than the steamers, but soldiered on, until the bridge opened. She is seen here at New Holland, with the visiting *Waverley* lying off awaiting the pontoon.

102. The little *Bilsdale,* built in 1900, ended a somewhat chequered career at Scarborough, not being broken up until 1935. Excursion steamers were not common in the water between here and the Forth, our next port of call.

102

103. The main Forth operator prior to the First World War was the Galloway Saloon Steam Packet Co. It later came under North British Railway control, but the *Wemyss Castle* built as *Gareloch* in 1872 for the NB Clyde fleet was sold to them in 1891. She was of typical raised quarterdeck design with oscillating engine, and lasted in Galloway service until 1906.

104. The Redcliffe Shipping Co., of Hull moved onto the Forth Cruising scene in 1934, and one of the vessels used for two seasons was *Fusilier*; see plate 45. She was later sold to Blackpool owners.

105. The Redcliffe Co., also operated the former Humber ferry *Brocklesby* for two seasons as the *Highland Queen*. With appearance improved by a new funnel, she is seen here at Leith in 1936. She also only operated for two seasons being sold for breaking at the end of 1936.

105

107

106 to 108. The Grangemouth and Forth Towing Company had previously used their tugs on a limited programme of excursions, but in 1927 they bought the Clyde Steamer *Isle of Skye*, built as *Madge Wildfire* for Captain Campbell in 1886 at McKnight's Yard in Ayr. She subsequently sailed for the CSP Co., and later for Captain Buchanan, when her name was first changed.

She became *Fair Maid* on the Forth, and offered a variety of sailings from Leith to Aderdour and Kirkcaldy. She also sailed occasionally from Grangemouth. She was the last excursion steamer left on the Forth and in 1939 her cruising ceased; she returned to the Clyde for war service, and never again carried passengers apart from standing in for *Lucy Ashton* for a short spell. She was scrapped in 1945.

Our views show her at Aberdour (plate 106); under repair at Grangemouth (plate 107); and entering Leith Harbour (plate 108).

108

110

111

109. The most common form of paddle steamer propulsion in the latter part of the nineteenth century was the single diagonal engine. The example shown here belongs to the steamer illustrated on the previous page —*Madge Wildfire.* Usually combined with the haystack type of boiler this unit could be found on many vessels.

Unlike continental designs, where the engines are almost hidden from view, the Clyde vessels of the latter part of the nineteenth century had engines in full view of the passengers from the alleyways of the main deck. There, one could watch the 'chief' fighting with the levers as the captain rang orders down from the bridge via the engine room telegraph. Fighting was the operative word with single diagonal engines, as most had a slip eccentric to work the slide valve, and on leaving a pier the engineer had to operate the valve gear by hand until the approximate moment was reached when it was locked in position and the engine crankshaft provided the movement.

Many single diagonal engines were also fitted with a starting engine to move the crank should the engine get stuck on top or bottom dead centre. A characteristic of vessels fitted with such engines was the two and fro surging motion when the vessel was travelling at speed.

Needless to say, simple engines were expensive to run once coal costs started to rise. A few engines were produced as tandem compounds, that is both cylinders in tandem driving the same single crank.

110. The Caledonian Steam Packet Co., were always in the forefront of paddle steamer development, and the engines of the *Duchess of Montrose* were no exception. They illustrate the twin crank arrangement found on most vessels from the eighteen nineties onwards, but in fact are triple expansion, with two high pressure cylinders, one in tandem with the intermediate pressure one, and one in tandem with the low pressure one, whereas single diagonal engines usually worked at no more than 50 psi. The trend was set with triple expansion and compound engines to higher boiler pressures. The CSP Co., in general, used navy type boilers in a closed stokehold where the draught was created by steam driven fans in the engine rooms, and the stokehold entry was via air locks. Boiler pressures were now 150-200 psi. The cranks were set at 90 degrees, and still gave some surging motion.

Surface condensers were in almost universal use from the turn of the century, and by the time the steam had done its work, and an engine driven or independent air pump had extracted the last out of the condensate, it was quite possible for over 20" of vacuum to be recorded. The condensate was then returned to the boiler via a hot well and steam driven feed pumps. It was usual for most auxiliaries to be run on exhaust steam from the main engine, including air pump (if independent), feed pumps, ballast and fire pumps, and steam generators.

111. The Fairfield Company provided a powerful set of triple diagonal engines for the *Jeanie Deans* of 1931. These were copied when Rankin and Blackmore built their engines for *Waverley* and *Bristol Queen.* Steam in all cases was supplied by a double ended scotch boiler, with furnaces at each end, requiring the use of two uptakes.

With cranks at 180 degrees, the triple crank engine gave a smooth passage. Originally coal fired, *Jeanie Deans* was converted to burn oil in 1956 /57.

112. The funnels make the ship. This view of *Waverley* taken in 1962 shows her with two odd funnels, the forward one is all welded, a replacement in the winter of 1961 /62, and the after is the original rivetted one with the hoop still visible to suit the LNER funnel colours. It was replaced in the winter of 1962 /63.

112

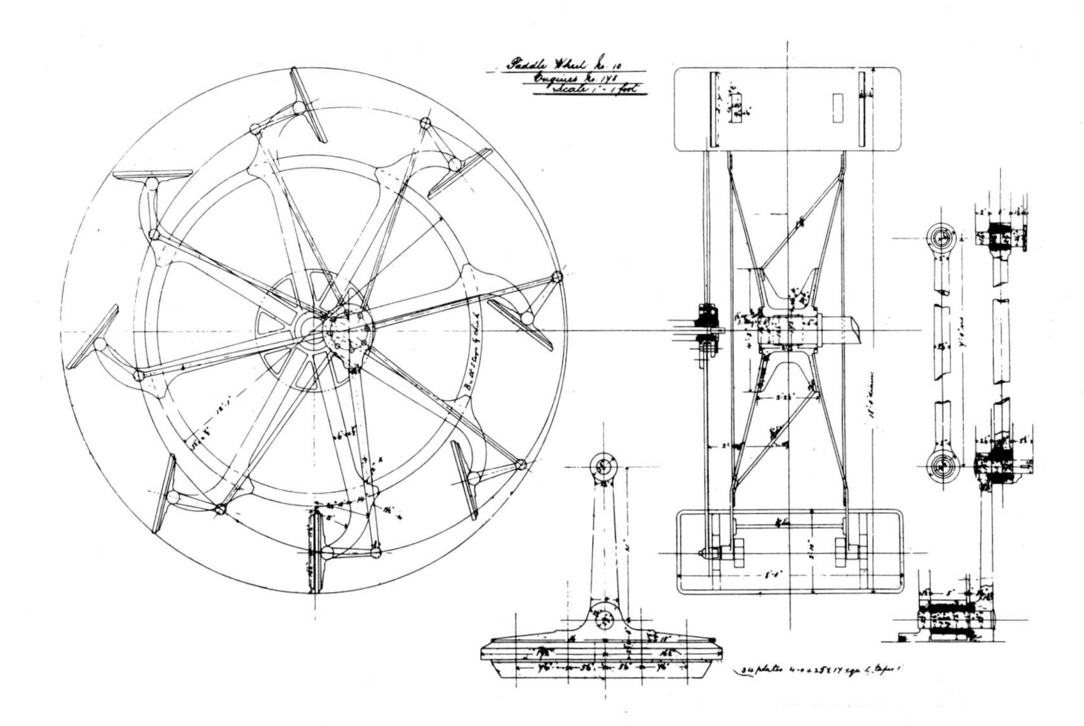

PADDLE WHEELS

The normal pattern of paddle wheels fitted to most of the ships illustrated in this book were of the feathering variety, that is to say that the floats were angled by mechanical means to enter and leave the water at a shallow angle. Much experimentation took place in the early days to find the best angle of entry and withdrawal. William Stroudley, the Chief Mechanical Engineer, of the London, Brighton and South Coast Railway developed a design of rimless wheel for the cross-channel steamers of that railway, although he was basically a locomotive engineer! This was subsequently copied by numerous shipyards and modified to suit the needs of smaller vessels.

A typical rimless wheel as fitted to the North British fleet is shown above. The floats were of Canadian Rock Elm. This design of wheel was fitted right up to the last ship to be built — *Waverley*. By the turn of the century the pin centres had been standardised at 14'10". Whilst most of the ships had flat floats, *Jeanie Deans* of 1931 had curved ones which gave less power astern, and *Talisman* of 1935 originally had curved steel floats, but these were soon replaced by flat wooden ones. The 1906 *Marmion* had smaller diameter wheels.

The Caledonian Steam Packet Co., preferred the rimmed type of wheel with curved steel floats, usually seven to each wheel. The 1934 *Caledonia* had her wheels rebuilt to take 8 floats however following vibration in service. The South Coast fleets tended also to follow the rimmed design and use steel floats which were said to be more durable in the heavier seas encountered in the Channel!

There were advantages with the wooden float. If an obstacle was hit it usually smashed the float without doing much damage to the running gear; with steel floats it could bend the whole paddle arm assembly.

The characteristic paddle beat, now only heard from *Waverley*, is far more pronounced with straight wooden floats.

Acknowledgements

Firstly, thanks must go to Allan Brown, who provided the lions share of the prints which make up this collection, and the slides for the cover. Secondly my good friend Gavin Johnston allowed me to dip into his extensive albums for further shots.

The photographic credits are as follows:

Allan Brown: Plates 58, 61, 62, 63, 83, 98, 110.

Allan Brown Collection: Plates 2, 15, 33, 36, 38, 47, 49, 52, 59, 69, 70, 71, 73, 87, 91, 102, 103.

B.C. Bending: Plate 76. J. Goss: Plates 41, 97, 100. G. Reed: Plate 101. I. McMillan Collection: Plate 51. A. G. Taylor Collection: Plate 46. The late C. Lawson Kerr: Plates 35, 39, 99. Stromer /Vogt Collection: Plates 8, 10, 11, 12, 28, 45.

G. Johnston Collection: 1, 3, 4, 5, 6, 7, 9, 13, 14, 23, 25, 32, 34, 37, 43, 44, 66, 88, 93, 112.

The late Fred A. Plant: Plates 16, 17, 18, 19, 20, 21, 22, 24, 27, 29, 30, 31, 42, 48, 50, 53, 54, 55, 56, 57, 60, 65, 67, 68, 72, 74, 75, 77, 78, 79, 81, 82, 84, 85, 86, 89, 90, 92, 104, 105, 107, 108.

Author's Collection: Plates 40, 80, 94, 95, 96. Unknown: Plates 26, 64, 106, 109, 111.